PHILADELPHIA
The Delaplaine
2021 Long Weekend Guide

No business listed in this guide has provided *anything* free to be included.

Andrew Delaplaine

Senior Editors
Renee & Sophie Delaplaine
Senior Writer
James Cubby

Gramercy Park Press
New York London Paris

WANT 3 FREE THRILLERS?

Why, of course you do!

If you like these writers--
Vince Flynn, Brad Thor, Tom Clancy, James Patterson,
David Baldacci, John Grisham, Brad Meltzer, Daniel
Silva, Don DeLillo
If you like these TV series –
House of Cards, Scandal, West Wing, The Good Wife,
Madam Secretary, Designated Survivor

You'll love the **unputdownable** series about
Jack Houston St. Clair, with political intrigue, romance
and loads of action and suspense.

Besides writing travel books, I've written political thrillers for many
years that have delighted hundreds of thousands of readers. I want to
introduce you to my work!
Send me an email and I'll send you a link where you can download the
first 3 books in my bestselling series, **absolutely FREE.**

Mention **this book** when you email me.
andrewdelaplaine@mac.com

PHILADELPHIA
The Delaplaine
Long Weekend Guide

TABLE OF CONTENTS

Chapter 1
WHY PHILADELPHIA?

Philadelphia is one of the most popular cities in the U.S. for visitors. Philadelphia is also one of the most historic cities in America as it's home to the Liberty Bell and Independence Hall, where the Constitution and the Declaration of Independence were signed. Philadelphia, known as the City of

Brotherly Love, is also the sixth largest city in the U.S. so there's obviously much to do and see. Some call the city the birthplace of life, liberty and the pursuit of happiness and most believe it lives up to that slogan.

Philadelphia is overflowing with history and if you're visiting here are the attractions that you should not miss. **The Liberty Bell**, located on Market Street, is the symbol of freedom and this cracked bell is a historical gem. **Independence Hall**, on Chestnut Street, offers guided tours and visitors get to see where the Declaration of Independence was signed. The **National Constitution Center**, on Arch Street, offers a variety exhibitions and shows about the U.S. Constitution and American history.

Franklin Court, on Market Street, is the site of where Benjamin Franklin's house once stood and there you'll find a museum with a print shop, a post office where you can send letters hand-stamped with Franklin's original postmark. **Elfreth's Alley**, the oldest residential street in America, features a museum with several historic houses. **The Betsy Ross House**, a 250-year old house furnished as it was during Betsy Ross's time, features artifacts and history about the famous flag maker. **Christ Church & Christ Church Burial Ground**, founded in 1695, is the church where man of America's leaders worshiped and the graveyard where many are buried. American Philosophical Society Museum is a museum that celebrates the Society, founded in 1743 by Benjamin Franklin. Carpenter's Hall, the site of the meeting of the First Continental Congress in 1774, is a popular stop for history buffs. The

Declaration House, also known as the Graff House, is the setting where Thomas Jefferson wrote the Declaration of Independence in 1776.

Philadelphia, besides its historical significance, is home to many outstanding art museums such as the Rodin Museum. The **Rodin Museum** opened in 1929 and boasts the largest collection of sculptor Auguste Rodin's works outside Paris. The **Barnes Foundation**, located on the Benjamin Franklin Parkway, houses one of the world's leading collections of French Impressionist and Post-Impressionist paintings. The **Pennsylvania Academy of the Fine Arts**, located in a historic Center City building, houses a masterful collection of American art. **The Philadelphia Museum of Art**, located at the end of the Benjamin Franklin Parkway, covers 10 acres and houses an immense collection of more than

300,000 works of art. Philadelphia also is home to The Franklin Institute Science Museum, one of the oldest science museums in the country, a museum filled with exhibits honoring the life and work of Benjamin Franklin. The African American Museum in Philadelphia, located in the historic district, is a celebration of African American history and culture. The University of Pennsylvania Museum of Archaeology and Anthropology, known as the Penn Museum, is dedicated to the world's cultural heritage featuring exhibits like the 12-ton Egyptian sphinx.

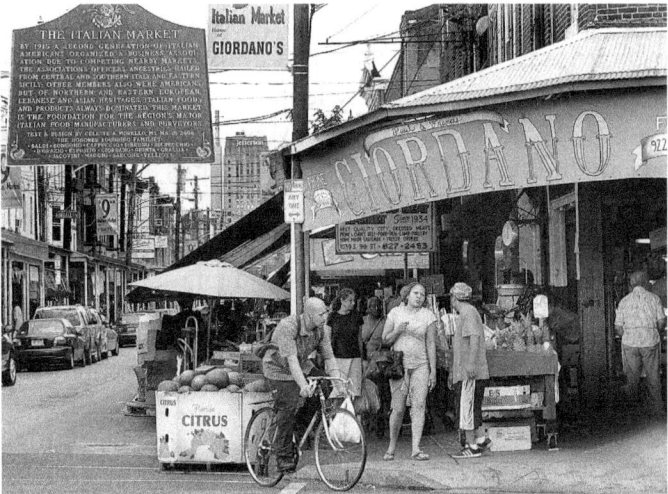

While touring Philadelphia here are a few interesting spots that should not be missed. The **Italian Market** is America's oldest outdoor market made famous by the film *Rocky*. **The Philadelphia Zoo,** America's first zoo, houses some of the world's most fascinating animals. The Avenue of the Arts, touted by Billy Crystal in commercials, is where you'll find the Philadelphia Orchestra at the Kimmel Center, the Wilma Theater and the Pennsylvania Academy of Fine Arts. Eastern State Penitentiary, a haunting prison with a Haunted House, offers daily tours to those interesting in see where infamous criminals like Al Capone were held captive. Of course a visit to Philadelphia is not complete without a visit to the "Rocky" steps, the steps to the Philadelphia Art Museum, a favorite of visitors who don't even visit the museum.

Shoppers will have no trouble spending their money in Philadelphia with its wealth of shopping malls, boutiques, and specialty shops. Rittenhouse Square in Center City offers an impressive selection of upscale shops. Old City features a variety of hip boutiques and vintage shops. Main Street Manayunk, an alternative to mall shopping, features a variety of local shops and national chains. South Street, located between Center City and South Philly, offers a unique and eclectic selection of shops and tattoo parlors.

Take your appetite when you visit Philadelphia as it's packed with some of the best restaurants in the country but while there you must sample the classic Philly cheese steak sandwich. Reading Terminal, a historic food court in Center City, is a food lovers' paradise filled with aromas and fresh produce, Amish specialties, meats, seafood, and poultry.

Philadelphia isn't known for its nightlife but there are some interesting low-key bars and nightclubs. The best area for nightlife is around Rittenhouse Square and Old City. You'll also find some clubs around South Street. Philly is known for its live music and there's a wealth of live music venues offering everything from rock to hip hop.

Philadelphia sports fans are very loyal as Philadelphia is home to the Eagles, Phillies, Flyers, 76ers and Wings, all teams that play their home games in the South Philadelphia Sports Complex section of the city.

Chapter 2
GETTING ABOUT

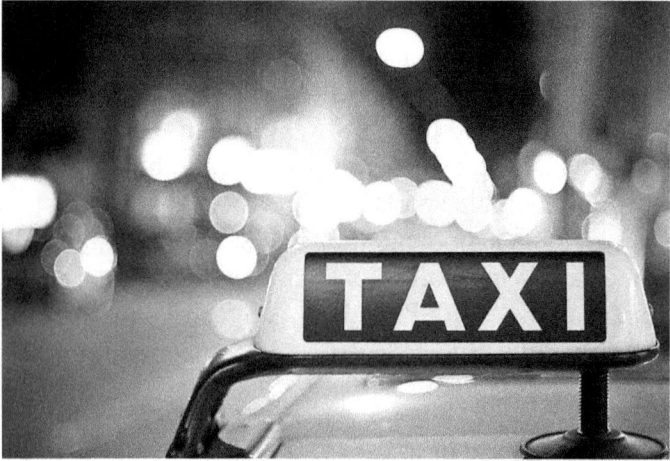

I would never bring a car into Philadelphia. If you have a car, the best thing to do is find someplace cheap to park it (at the end of the subway lines out of town, let's say) and rely on the rather good public transportation during your visit. Trains, buses and trolleys all converge at a couple of main terminals, the 69th Street Transportation Center and the 30th Street Station. The most minor parking violation is result in a ticket. The meter maids in Philadelphia are some of the most relentless vultures in America.

The Southeastern Pennsylvania Transportation Authority is responsible for the different modes of transport in the city and suburbs, including the

Regional Rail lines, the Market-Frankfort Line, the Broad Street Line, the Trolley system and Buses.

Complete information on each of these services, as well as day passes and other costs, can be found at their web site:

www.septa.org

Again, strongly urge you to avail yourself of this excellent system.

If you don't want to hassle with public transport, there are plenty of taxis available.

OTHER TOURIST INFORMATION
www.visitphilly.com

Chapter 3
WHERE TO STAY

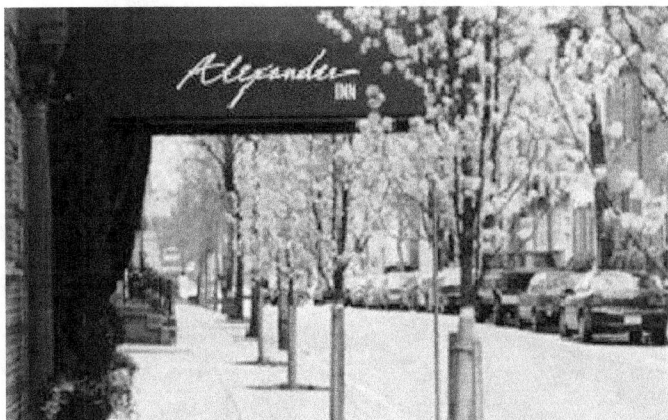

ALEXANDER INN
301 South 12th St. (at Spruce St.), Philadelphia: 215-923-3535
www.alexanderinn.com
NEIGHBORHOOD: Washington Square West
For an affordable stay in the city center, the 48-room Alexander Inn is a homey, unpretentious place to stay.

CORNERSTONE B&B

3300 Baring St, Philadelphia, 215-387-6065
www.cornerstonebandb.com
NEIGHBORHOOD: University City
A family-owned B&B set in an 1865 house featuring six guest rooms. Amenities: complimentary Wi-Fi, flat-screen TVs, complimentary breakfast and antique furnishings. Facilities include: spa tub and garden. Conveniently located near attractions like the Philadelphia Museum of Art.

HOTEL MONACO

433 Chestnut St., Philadelphia: 215-925-2111
www.monaco-philadelphia.com
This is a Kimpton property, and they seem to have some of the more exciting hotels wherever I run into them. There's always something going on in the public areas that make their hotels hip and trendy. Here, they overlook Independence Hall and the Liberty Bell in a great location, situated in a

renovated Greek Revival building dating back to 1907, so the "bones" are very impressive in this structure. They offer a nightly wine hour and have a fitness room. The hip and trendy I mentioned? You'll find all that going on up on the rooftop bar, called **Stratus**, which attracts a lot of local hipsters, so it's always busy. The **Red Owl Tavern** is the restaurant off the lobby. The Fifth Street subway is 3 or 4 minutes by foot, so cabbing it is the best option unless you're walking anyway.

INDEPENDENT HOTEL
1234 Locust St, Philadelphia, 215-772-1440
www.theindependenthotel.com
NEIGHBORHOOD: Midtown Village

Boutique hotel featuring 24 luxurious guest rooms in a restored Georgian-Revival building. Amenities: complimentary Wi-Fi, flat-screen TVs, microwaves and mini-fridges. Complimentary continental breakfast delivered daily. Facilities: Fitness Center with Gym, Workout Room and onsite Italian Restaurant Bar/Lounge. Complimentary evening wine and cheese reception. Conveniently located near attractions like: Independence Hall, the Liberty Bell, and Rittenhouse.

LA RESERVE
1804 Pine St, Philadelphia, 215-735-1137
www.lareservebandb.com
NEIGHBORHOOD: Rittenhouse Square
Consisting of two beautiful, well-preserved 1850's four-story townhouses with 15 guestrooms. Amenities: complimentary Wi-Fi, cable TV and complimentary hot or continental breakfast. Note: four story hotel without an elevator. Conveniently located within walking distance to local shopping, restaurants and major Philadelphia historic attractions.

LE MERIDIEN HOTEL
1421 Arch St., Philadelphia. 215-422-8200
www.marriott.com
It's hard to believe that this gorgeous modern hotel property right in the heart of town was once-upon-a-time a YMCA? After you take a take in the ornately carved woodwork and the high ceilings, you'll see it looks more like a Gilded Age mansion than a Y. But the modern furnishings work quite well with the 19th century building.

MORRIS HOUSE
225 S 8th St, Philadelphia, 215-922-2446
www.morrishousehotel.com
NEIGHBORHOOD: Washington Square Park
Located in a 1787 colonial home, this upscale boutique hotel offers beautifully decorated rooms featuring Victorian furnishings. Amenities: complimentary Wi-Fi, flat-screen TVs, and iPod docks. Complimentary continental breakfast and

afternoon cookies. Conveniently located blocks from historic attractions. On-site restaurant.

PENN'S VIEW HOTEL
14 N Front St, Philadelphia, 215-922-7600
www.pennsviewhotel.com
NEIGHBORHOOD: Market Street
Overlooking Market Street, this historic Old City hotel features traditional rooms. Amenities: complimentary Wi-Fi, color TV, and complimentary continental breakfast. Fitness room. Conveniently located near attractions like Betsy Ross House, Penn's Landing and the Liberty Bell.

RITTENHOUSE
210 W Rittenhouse Square, Philadelphia, 215-546-9000
www.rittenhousehotel.com
NEIGHBORHOOD: Rittenhouse Square
Located across from Rittenhouse Square Park, this upscale 118-room hotel has received both the Forbes

Four Star and AAA Five Diamond ratings, which is why I usually stay here when someone else is footing the bill. (Here or the Ritz.) Amenities: complimentary Wi-Fi, flat-screen TVs, iPod docks, overnight shoeshine, newspaper delivery, and complimentary car service. Facilities: gym, indoor pool, steam room and sauna, four on-site dining options and a cocktail bar. Walking distance to shopping restaurants, and business district.

RITZ-CARLTON

10 Ave of The Arts, Philadelphia, 215-523-8000
www.ritzcarlton.com/en/hotels/philadelphia
NEIGHBORHOOD: Rittenhouse Square, Penn Center

Located across from Philadelphia City Hall, this luxury hotel offers 299 guest rooms and suites. Amenities: Wi-Fi (fee), flat-screen TVs, iPod docks, and marble bathrooms. Facilities: high-end American bistro/bar in the domed lobby, upscale spa and fitness center.

SOFITEL
120 S 17th St, Philadelphia, 215-569-8300
www.sofitel-philadelphia.com
NEIGHBORHOOD: Rittenhouse Square, Penn Center
Luxury hotel mixing French elegance with American style features 308 guestrooms and suites.
Amenities: complimentary Wi-Fi, flat-screen TVs, and marble bathrooms. Facilities: fitness center, on-site brasserie, stylish French restaurant/bar and a fitness center. Located near Philadelphia's French Quarter and steps away from local attractions,

shopping and restaurants. Just a 10-minute walk to the Kimmel Center for the Performing Arts.

THOMAS BOND HOUSE
129 S 2nd St, Philadelphia, 215-923-8523
www.thomasbondhousebandb.com
NEIGHBORHOOD: Old City
Elegant restored 4-story 1769 B&B featuring 12 guestrooms, located in Independence National Historic Park. Amenities: complimentary Wi-Fi, cable TV, period furniture and continental breakfast. Just steps away from historic landmarks. Non-smoking venue.

Chapter 4
WHERE TO EAT

A.KITCHEN
135 S 18th St, Philadelphia, 215-825-7030
www.akitchenandbar.com
CUISINE: American (New)
DRINKS: Full Bar
SERVING: Breakfast, Lunch, & Dinner
PRICE RANGE: $$$
NEIGHBOROOD: Rittenhouse Square, Penn Center
Stylish bistro with a creative seasonal small plate
menu created by award-winning Chef Eli Kulp. Menu
favorites include: Grilled Rabbit and Fried Oysters.
Great atmosphere with outdoor tables – great for
people watching.

ABE FISHER
1623 Sansom St, Philadelphia, 215-867-0088
www.abefisherphilly.com
CUISINE: Modern European
DRINKS: Full Bar
SERVING: Dinner

PRICE RANGE: $$$
NEIGHBOROOD: Rittenhouse Square, Penn Center
Jewish-themed bistro/pub. Menu picks include:
Salmon Gravlax and a Corned Pork Belly Reuben that
is a marvelous twist on the Reuben you grew up
expecting.

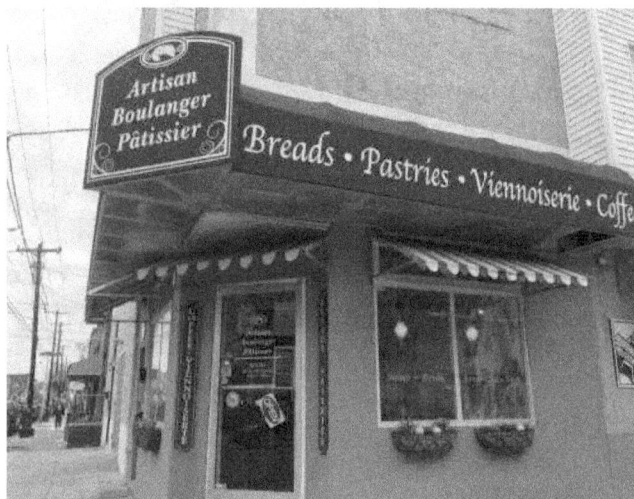

ARTISAN BOULANGER PATISSIER
1218 Mifflin St, Philadelphia: 215-271-4688
CUISINE: Bakery
DRINKS: No Alcohol
SERVING: Breads, Desserts
In the South Philadelphia East Passyunk
neighborhood you'll find French-trained Cambodian
émigré André Chin whipping up some of the best
croissants in town, featuring flavors like aux almond,
pain au chocolat, or spinach, mushroom and ricotta.

AMADA
217 Chestnut St, Philadelphia, 215-625-2450
https://philadelphia.amadarestaurant.com/
CUISINE: Tapas Bar/Spanish
DRINKS: Full Bar
SERVING: Lunch & Dinner
PRICE RANGE: $$$
NEIGHBORHOOD: Old City
Contemporary Spanish eatery featuring a modern twist on tapas. It's got a cozy atmosphere, with tables against the high windows looking out onto the quaint street here in the Old City. Nothing fancy inside—just rough wooden tables. The bar is a little awkward—it's slightly higher than it needs to be for comfort, as if someone mis-measured when they built it. There's a wall with lanterns lined up, and it makes you think instantly of Paul Revere; I don't know why, but it does. Maybe it's the high glass doors you pass through when you walk in, giving the place a very Colonial "tavern" feel. It's all about the food anyway, with sides of cured ham hanging from the ceiling. Roast suckling pig and Lobster paella are specialties, and boy, they are scumptious. Other Favorites: Tortilla Espanola tapas, Bacon-wrapped dates, and Octopus tapas. Great place for sharing.

ALPEN ROSE
116 S 13th St, Philadelphia, 215-600-0709
https://www.alpenrosephl.com/
CUISINE: Steakhouse/Seafood
DRINKS: Full Bar
SERVING: Dinner
PRICE RANGE: $$$$

NEIGHBORHOOD: Midtown Village
Upscale steakhouse with a very warm interior enhanced by a wall of shelves filled with books (lighted quite dramatically). Chandeliers hang from above, glittering from the barrel-vaulted wooden ceiling, complementing the brick walls. Choose between booth seating and tables in the open room. The focus is on a wide-selection of meats butchered and dry-aged in house. Favorites: Tuna carpaccio or bone marrow toast to start; Veal or Pork Tomahawk. All the best cuts are represented: strip steak (18 oz), Porterhouse (32 oz), Rib Eye (bone in at 24 oz, bone out, 18 oz), as well as a NY strip, bone in or out. Steak just melts in your mouth. You barely need a fork to cut it. Don't like steak? They have a nice selection of alternatives. Great cocktails. Limited seating. Reservations recommended

BARBUZZO
110 S 13th St, Philadelphia, 215-546-9300
www.barbuzzo.com
CUISINE: Mediterranean
DRINKS: Full Bar
SERVING: Lunch & Dinner
PRICE RANGE: $$$
NEIGHBORHOOD: Market East, Avenue of the Arts, South
This little restaurant has a budino dessert that people told me is fabulous. I checked it out myself, and it is.

BISTRO ROMANO

120 Lombard St., 215-925-8880
www.bistroromano.com
CUISINE: Italian
DRINKS: Full bar
SERVING: Dinner daily
PRICE RANGE: $$$

Big piles of Italian food served up in a very commercial atmosphere. But it can be a lot of fun if you're with a crowd. It's in an 18th century granary, Bistro Romano is also home to the **Original Mystery Theatre**, a murder mystery dinner theatre with performances on Friday and Saturday nights. Bistro Romano's many honors include Philadelphia Magazine's Best of Philly award, CitySearch's Best Italian and Best Romantic, TV's Fox29 Philadelphia's Most Romantic Table and the Wine Spectator "Best of Award of Excellence."

BLUME

1500 Locust St, Philadelphia, 267-761-5582
www.blumephilly.com

CUISINE: American (New)
DRINKS: Full Bar
SERVING: Dinner, Brunch on Sat & Sun.
PRICE RANGE: $$
NEIGHBORHOOD: Rittenhouse

Popular hipster spot offering a creative menu of New American fare. You can't miss the big butterfly dominating the doors when you walk up. It's designed like a hippy dress or an old VW bus decorated with psychedelic designs from San Francisco in the 1970s, very cute. Inside, the décor is just as whimsical, with Broadway style lighted letters glued upside down to the ceiling, punctuated by a lot of lights hanging with plants. The word BLUME in bold white letters forms a repetitive motif on the walls. Menu picks: Gnocchi and New York Steak; nice selection of flatbreads—Avocado, Mushroom, Lobster, Pancetta, Margherita. If you go for brunch, get the mushroom grits or the shrimp & girts (as good as I've had in Charleston or Savannah). Impressive wine list and delicious cocktails. Happy hour.

BOTTLE BAR EAST

GOOD FOOD
KITCHEN OPEN LATE

BOTTLE BAR EAST
1308 Frankford, Philadelphia, 267-909-8867

www.bottlebareast.com
CUISINE: Gastropub
DRINKS: Full Bar
SERVING: Lunch, Dinner

PRICE RANGE: $$
NEIGHBORHOOD: Fishtown
This combination bar and retail store offers an impressive list of 700 varieties of craft beer, that's right—700 of them. The staff, all self-described "beer geeks," are very happy to share their knowledge of the many beers available. (Sometimes *too* happy.) The menu features a variety of "bar food" like a grilled Philly-style Cuban sandwich and Grilled cheese with apple butter.

BRIGANTESSA
1520 E Passyunk Ave, Philadelphia, 267-318-7341
https://www.brigantessaphila.com/
CUISINE: Italian
DRINKS: Full Bar
SERVING: Dinner, Sunday Brunch
PRICE RANGE: $$$
NEIGHBORHOOD: East Passyunk
Comfortable eatery in a simple brick building (with nice flower boxes hanging from the second floor) offering a simple menu of Southern Italian fare in a long narrow room with basic wooden tables and chairs. A bar is up front when you come in, giving you that option. (Given that option, I always take it, LOL.) Favorites: Rotisserie meats or their Wood-oven pizzas (their specialty), but also some good antipasti, like the wood-grilled octopus salad,

eggplant croquetas, risotto fritters with speck (delicious), meat balls using beef & pork. Several nicely prepared pastas also available.

THE CAPITAL GRILLE
1338 Chestnut St., 215-545-9588
www.thecapitalgrille.com
CUISINE: Steakhouse
DRINKS: Full bar
SERVING: Mon- Fri lunch and dinner, Sat – Sun dinner only
PRICE RANGE: $$$$
I know it's a chain, but the one here seems to me to be better than any of the others. Why? Don't know. Maybe it's the opulent setting.

CHEU FISHTOWN
1416 Frankford Ave, 267-758-2269
www.cheufishtown.com
CUISINE: Noodles/Asian Fusion
DRINKS: Full Bar
SERVING: Lunch & Dinner
PRICE RANGE: $$
NEIGHBORHOOD: Fishtown
Situated in what used to be an old horse barn is this hip, fun and creative ramen bar with murals painted by local artists, a craft beer list on the reclaimed marquee sign. Has a delicious menu of Asian bites like Fried chicken buns, Corn Rangoon, Brisket ramen with kimchi and Shumai. Small space so it gets crowded. Nice selection of beers and wine.

CHIMA BRAZILIAN STEAKHOUSE
1901 John F. Kennedy Blvd., 215-525-3233
www.chima.cc
CUISINE: Brazilian, Barbecue, Steakhouse
DRINKS: Full bar
SERVING: Dinner daily
PRICE RANGE: $$$
Located in the Center City, you get the full rodizio
dinner served by authentic Gauchos. If you're not into
doing the whole experience, slip into their nice
lounge for a cocktail and appetizers. Great place to
conduct meetings.

CHUBBY CATTLE
146 N 10th St, Philadelphia, 866-622-8853
https://www.chubbycattle.com/chubby-cattle-philadelphia/
CUISINE: Chinese/Seafood/Mongolian
DRINKS: Full Bar
SERVING: Lunch & Dinner
PRICE RANGE: $$$
NEIGHBORHOOD: Chinatown
Conveyer belt-based hotspot with a healthy menu of "reformed traditional" Mongolian cuisine. (which means, don't expect any char-broiled yak). You order on an iPad, pull ingredients off a moving conveyer line and your meal will come back to you shortly. Once you get used to it, it's fun. Famous for the high quality of their ingredients, like their homemade noodles. Favorites: A-5 Wagyu Beef and Lamb shank. You get your own pot with a choice of soup bases.

CITY TAVERN
138 S 2nd St, Philadelphia, 215-413-1443
www.citytavern.com
CUISINE: American (Traditional)/Comfort Food
DRINKS: Full bar
SERVING: Lunch & Dinner
PRICE RANGE: $$
NEIGHBORHOOD: Old City
Guests step back into the 18th century when entering this 4 story Colonial tavern dating back to 1772 (though it was restored after a fire in the 19th Century). Servers are dressed in period garb serving traditional American fare like Colonial turkey pot pie

and Roast duckling served with freshly baked bread made from Colonial recipes. Favorites: Turkey Stew and Beef Bourguignon. Sample beer made from recipes courtesy of Washington, Jefferson, Franklin and Hamilton. Even the serving plates, utensils, and the pewter goblets all seem from another era.

COTOLETTA FITLER SQUARE
2227 Pine St, Philadelphia, 267-519-9697
https://www.cotolettafs.com/
CUISINE: Italian
DRINKS: Full Bar
SERVING: Dinner, Brunch Sat & Sun.
PRICE RANGE: $$$
NEIGHBORHOOD: Fitler Square
What a pretty room! The wooden floors and wood slatted ceiling match so well with lavender colored chairs to give the long narrow room a charming and sophisticated, stylish yet comfortable atmosphere, which complements the rustic Italian comfort food on offer here. There's a daisy on every table, protruding from pre-used wine bottles pressed into service as makeshift vases. Bright and cheerful. Favorites: Sausages stuffed with Provolone; Meatballs with ricotta (so rich and tasty); Cioppino (get extra bread to dip into this specialty); excellent veal cutlets served in a variety of styles (Milanese, Parmesan, Piccata); Chicken parm; and Shrimp Scampi. Wednesday Happy Hour, but I think they ought to do one every weekday, like most places. Nice wine selection. Classic Italian desserts.

DAVIO'S NORTHERN ITALIAN STEAKHOUSE

111 S. 17th St., 215-563-4810
www.davios.com
CUISINE: Steakhouse, Italian
DRINKS: Full bar
SERVING: Mon – Fri breakfast, lunch, and dinner,
Sat – Sun dinner only
PRICE RANGE: $$$
Everything made by hand from the best ingredients.
You can get everything from aged steaks to simple-
yet-unique pasta creations. There are several of these
around the country, in Foxborough, and Atlanta and
Davio's Cucina in Chestnut Hill.

DEL FRISCO'S DOUBLE EAGLE STEAK HOUSE

1428-32 Chestnut St., 215-246-0533
www.delfriscos.com
CUISINE: Steakhouse, Seafood
DRINKS: Full bar
SERVING: Mon – Fri lunch and dinner, Sat – Sun
dinner only

PRICE RANGE: $$$$
NEIGHBOROOD: Rittenhouse Square
Del Frisco's is a dramatic restaurant covering multiple levels of the First Pennsylvania Bank building in Center City Philadelphia. They have a three-story wine tower looming over the main bar that dominates not only the room, but the conversation as well. Balconies flanked with bolts of red fabric overlook the sweeping main dining room. Downstairs boasts private dining and reception areas, including the Vault Room. Everybody who knows Del Frisco's knows it's all about the gorgeous dry-aged and hand-cut steaks (the usual wide selection of quality cuts you'd expect), but they also carry a lot of the best seafood, and occasionally some excellent, unusual starters, like the duck confit meatballs; fried calamari Shanghai-style; or the cheesesteak dumplings. Yum.

DIZENGOFF
1625 Sansom St, Philadelphia, 215-867-8181
www.dizengoffphilly.com
CUISINE: Middle Eastern
DRINKS: Beer & Wine Only
SERVING: Lunch, & Dinner
PRICE RANGE: $$
NEIGHBOROOD: Rittenhouse Square, Penn Center
Industrial designed eatery offering a variety of hummus – and only hummus along with fresh pita and Middle Eastern salads. The hummus topped with zucchini and za'atar is beyond delicious.

DOUBLE KNOT
120 S 13th St, Philadelphia, 215-631-3868

www.doubleknotphilly.com
CUISINE: Sushi Bar/Japanese
DRINKS: Full bar
SERVING: Dinner
PRICE RANGE: $$
NEIGHBORHOOD: Midtown village / Market East / Avenue of the Arts South
Comfortable Japanese eatery offering up a creative menu of sushi and robatayaki meats. During the day, they serve coffee, rice bowls and bahn mi. At night, things change. Try the Chef's Tasting Menu to get a full range of flavors. Menu picks: Broiled Seabass and Duck Scrapple Bao Buns. Creative cocktails like the Cheery Timber Hitch and the Double Knot.

ELA

627 S Third St, Philadelphia, 267-687-8512
www.elaphilly.com
CUISINE: American
DRINKS: Full Bar
SERVING: Dinner
PRICE RANGE: $$$
NEIGHBORHOOD: Queen Village
Chefs Jason Cichonski (say that 5 times in rapid succession) and Chip Roman joined forces to create ELA. The menu features innovative dishes like Scallop Noodles. The 6-Course Chefs' Tasting is a favorite because you can taste a wide assortment of their creative dishes and there's a lot of food. The bar menu is also creative and quite impressive on its own.

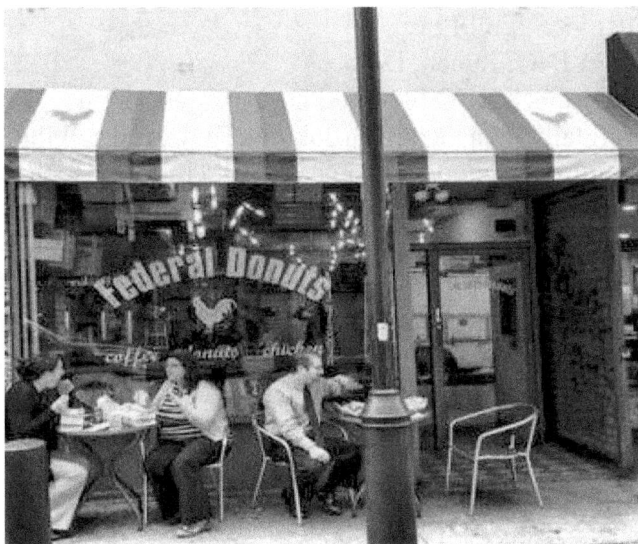

FEDERAL DONUTS
1219 S 2nd St., Philadelphia: 267-687-8258
www.federaldonuts.com
CUISINE: Donuts, American
DRINKS: No booze
SERVING: Breakfast, Lunch
The honey doughnuts are the big thing here. Chef
Michael Solomonov's version of fried chicken won
him the prestigious James Beard Award, but you have
to wait till 11:45 to order it. (He has a dry rub he uses,
such as buttermilk ranch.) Or you can get it with a
wet glaze (one version is honey-ginger and chili-
garlic).

FETTE SAU
1208 Frankford Ave., Philadelphia: 215-391-4888
www.fettesauphilly.com
CUISINE: American; BBQ

DRINKS: Full Bar
SERVING: Lunch, Dinner
Dry-rubbed BBQ is served here in a restaurant originally launched in Brooklyn. They even sell the meat by the pound so you can take a pile of it with you.

FOND
1537 S 11th St, Philadelphia, 215-551-5000
www.fondphilly.com
CUISINE: American (New)
DRINKS: Full Bar
SERVING: Dinner; closed Mondays
PRICE RANGE: $$$
NEIGHBOROOD: Passyunk Square
Casual eatery offers a menu of seasonal contemporary American cuisine. A couple of the owners used to work at the famous Le Bec Fin, so they know exactly what they're doing. Small but comfortable. Menu favorites include: Lobster and Strawberry salad and Pork belly. I am partial to the sweetbreads here. Delectable. Great selection of homemade breads & desserts.

FORK
306 Market St, Philadelphia, 215-625-9425
www.forkrestaurant.com
CUISINE: American
DRINKS: Full Bar
SERVING: Dinner & Brunch
PRICE RANGE: $$$
Contemporary American cuisine featuring house-made pastas and whole animal "feasts" served in a stylish bistro atmosphere.

HAN DYNASTY
3711 Market St., Philadelphia: 215-222-3711
www.handynasty.net
CUISINE: Chinese
DRINKS: Full Bar
SERVING: Lunch, Dinner
NEIGHBORHOOD: University City
Han Dynasty is a very popular local chain offering large portions suitable for families: rabbit with peanuts in chili oil; pork belly in garlic sauce, fried dumplings, scallion pancakes, pickled vegetables with pork, braised beef noodle soup. The dry pots are especially good—you get a sizzling mini wok with black mushrooms, bamboo shoots, bell peppers and Sichuan peppercorns and your choice of fish, lamb, beef, pork, rabbit, shrimp or chicken. Numerous other dishes and the atmosphere is fun and lively.

HIGH STREET ON MARKET
308 Market St, Philadelphia, 215-625-0988
www.highstreetonmarket.com
CUISINE: American (New)
DRINKS: Full Bar
SERVING: Breakfast, Lunch, & Dinner
PRICE RANGE: $$
NEIGHBOROOD: Old City
Chef Eli Kulp puts his touch on yet another local
eatery, this time with a country-chic décor. Menu
features edgy American fare that includes a variety of
sandwiches like the incredible grilled cheese and the
cured salmon sandwich. The on-site artisanal bakery
forms a very important part of the story here. This is
NOT a place for people who want to avoid carbs.
We've all had creative breakfast sandwiches, but try
the "Forager" – oyster mushrooms, kale that's been
lightly braised, a fried egg & Swiss cheese, topped
with a mushroom mayonnaise and all piled into a
delicious Kaiser roll. One dish I found particularly
creative was the caraway rye rigatoni served with
pastrami ragu. Wow!

ITV
1615 E Passyunk Ave, Philadelphia, 267-858-0669
www.itvphilly.com
CUISINE: Tapas/Small Plates
DRINKS: Full bar
SERVING: Dinner; closed Sun
PRICE RANGE: $$
NEIGHBORHOOD: East Passyunk Crossing

Comfortable eatery offering a variety of small plate dishes – New American cuisine with a French twist. ITV stands for In the Valley, the casual offshoot of Chef Nicholas Elmi's popular restaurant, **Laurel**, which is pretty hard to get into unless you book well ahead or show up the second they open. This is just next door. The place fills up early because of the popular Happy Hour menu. Bar features craft cocktails and an impressive wine selection. Start with smoked trout and trout roe that you slather over pumpernickel; then go for the whole chicken served with string beans and mushrooms—it's delightfully flavorful.

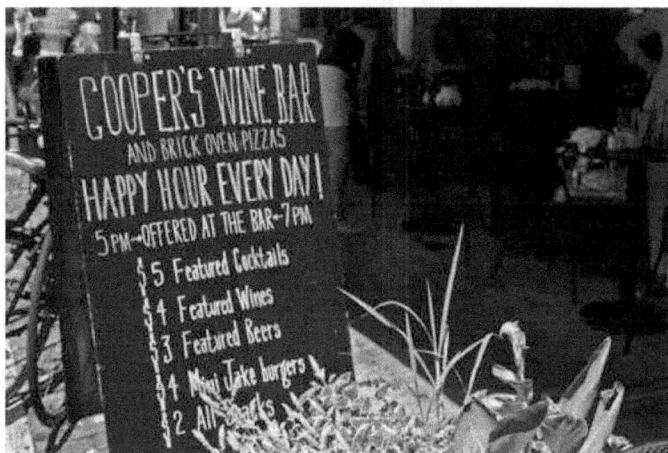

JAKE'S AND COOPER'S WINE BAR
4365 Main St., 215-483-0444
www.jakesandcoopers.com
CUISINE: American
DRINKS: Full bar

SERVING: Cooper's lunch and dinner, Sun brunch/ Jake's dinner daily, Sun brunch
PRICE RANGE: $$
The focus of Jake's and Cooper's is to have fantastic wines on hand. Wines have to complement their food and focus on the many terroirs. Labels are hand-selected by general manager Cosmo Mullen and chef Bruce Cooper, and the food menu stays true to its promise of sustainability without skimping on taste and texture. Need proof? Try the creamy Artichoke mac-and-cheese paired with Chapoutier's Cote du Rhone blanc.

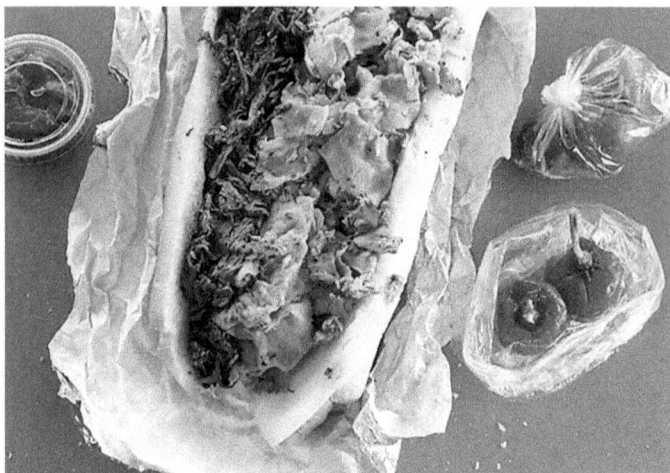

JOHN'S ROAST PORK
14 Snyder Ave, Philadelphia, 215-463-1951
www.johnsroastpork.com
CUISINE: Sandwiches
DRINKS: No Booze
SERVING: Breakfast, Lunch
PRICE RANGE: $

NEIGHBORHOOD: South Philly
This popular eatery is known as the "sandwich champion of Philadelphia." Menu favorites include Philly Cheesesteak and Roast Beef sandwiches. The places advertizes that it's the home of the "ultimate cheesesteak" so you know it better be good. For early risers, there's a nice selection of breakfast sandwiches at unbelievably low prices.

LAUREL
1617 E Passyunk Ave, Philadelphia, 215-271-8299
www.restaurantlaurel.com
CUISINE: French/American (New)
DRINKS: No Booze, but BYOB is encouraged
SERVING: Dinner; closed Sun & Mon
PRICE RANGE: $$$$
NEIGHBOROOD: East Passyunk Crossing
Small stylish eatery offering an impressive menu of French and American cuisine. Named one of the "25 Most Outstanding Restaurants of 2015" by GQ magazine. BYOB. Reservations recommended.

LE VIRTU
1927 E. Passyunk Ave, Philadelphia, 215-271-5626
www.levirtu.com
CUISINE: Italian
DRINKS: Full Bar
SERVING: Dinner
PRICE RANGE: $$$
Authentic Abruzzo-style Italian cuisine mainly sourced from local ingredients.

THE LOVE
130 S 18th St, 215-433-1555

www.theloverestaurant.com
CUISINE: American (New)
DRINKS: Full Bar
SERVING: Lunch & Dinner
PRICE RANGE: $$$
NEIGHBORHOOD: Rittenhouse Square, Penn Center
Neighborhood eatery with a charming farmhouse atmosphere that looks like an expert designer put some time in here. Offers a creative menu of seasonal American fare. Favorites: Brisket Pappardelle,Ricotta Ravioli, Fried chicken that's particularly good, Parker house rolls. Be sure to try the Mississippi comeback sauce. Reservations recommended.

MARRA'S
1734 E Passyunk Ave, Philadelphia, 215-463-9249
www.marrasone.com
CUISINE: Italian
DRINKS: Full Bar
SERVING: Lunch, & Dinner; closed Mon
PRICE RANGE: $$
NEIGHBOROOD: East Passyunk Crossing
Open since 1927, this old-school Italian eatery serves up Italian classics and brick-oven pizzas. Delicious lasagna, scampi, salmon, and pizza keep the regulars coming back.

MIDDLE CHILD
248 S 11th St, 267-930-8344
www.middlechildphilly.com
CUISINE: Breakfast/Sandwiches
DRINKS: No Booze

SERVING: Breakfast & Lunch
PRICE RANGE: $
NEIGHBORHOOD: Washington Square West
Super delicious sandwich spot around the Jefferson
hospital. It's a casual spot for daytime eats inspired
by classic diners and delis, plus pantry items to take
home. Lots of Eagles motif items decorate the walls.
They make everything fresh to order, so it takes a
while. But totally worth it to chill in line, and then
picnic outside. I ordered a hoisin eggplant sandwich
and the bread was baked/toasted to perfection while
the sandwich was exploding with flavor. Also the
"Phoagie" sandwich is a specialty – the classic Philly
sandwich with a Vietnam-vegan twist. Highly
recommend.

MR. MARTINO'S TRATTORIA
1646 E Passyunk Ave, Philadelphia, 215-755-0663
No Website
CUISINE: Italian
DRINKS: No Booze; BYOB allowed
SERVING: Dinner: Open Fri, Sat & Sun only
PRICE RANGE: $$ / **cash only**
NEIGHBOROOD: East Passyunk Crossing
Old-school Italian eatery with a European
atmosphere. Favorites include the Ravioli with red
sauce. Variety of vegetarian options. Cash only.
Weekend nights only

MONK'S CAFE
264 S 16th St., Philadelphia: 215-545-7005
www.monkscafe.com
CUISINE: Pubs, Belgian, Gastropubs
DRINKS: Full Bar
SERVING: Lunch, Dinner
NEIGHBORHOOD: Rittenhouse Square
In what looks like a little dive bar and tavern with a superior beer list they serve 8 types mussels & frites— including the De Koninck (De Koninck Ale, apples, Gruyère, caramelized leeks and garlic) and the Red Light (Hoegaarden, fumé, chile de arbol peppers, chervil and garlic).

NATIONAL MECHANICS
22 S 3rd St., Philadelphia: 215-701-4883
www.nationalmechanics.com
CUISINE: Pubs, American
DRINKS: Full Bar
SERVING: Lunch, Dinner

On the weekends, they lay out a massive Bloody Mary Bar with more hot sauces to choose from than you can name. Other items include bacon vodka (does that sound sick, or what?) or jalapeño tequila. The Gothic building is gorgeous, dating back to 1837. A collection of bottles going back decades hangs from the ceiling. Really fun place.

NOORD EETCAFE
1046 E Tasker St, Philadelphia, 267-909-9704
www.noordphilly.com
CUISINE: American, Scandinavian
DRINKS: No Booze; BYOB
SERVING: Dinner
PRICE RANGE: $$
Northern European cuisine expertly prepared and served.

OYSTER HOUSE
1516 Sansom St, Philadelphia, 215-567-7683
www.oysterhousephilly.com
CUISINE: Seafood
DRINKS: Full bar
SERVING: Lunch & Dinner; closed Sun
PRICE RANGE: $$
NEIGHBORHOOD: Rittenhouse Square, Penn Center
This is a seafood lover's dream in a décor that features high-top tables, lots of white tile, a marble bar. Open since 1976, this eatery offers a variety of fresh seafood – everything from fresh oysters (check out their Happy Hour Oysters at "a buck a shuck"), lobster, shrimp, cod, and salmon. Favorites: Salmon

burger and Seared Cod. Fans of New England clam chowder won't be disappointed.

THE PIAZZA AT SCHMIDT'S
1001 N 2ND ST, Philadelphia, 215-987-5986
www.livepiazza.com
CUISINE: Variety
DRINKS: Full Bar
SERVING: Lunch & Dinner
PRICE RANGE: $$
In Northern Liberties is a redeveloped brewery site perfect for a relaxed evening out. Visitors can watch a Philadelphia sports team on the big screen or browse a diverse array of shops.

PIZZERIA BEDDIA
1313 North Lee St, Philadelphia, 267-928-2256
https://www.pizzeriabeddia.com/
CUISINE: Pizza
DRINKS: Full Bar
SERVING: Dinner
PRICE RANGE: $$
NEIGHBORHOOD: Fishtown
Small pizza eatery with daily pie specials. It looks pretty bare and spartan when you come in here, almost like the dining hall on a college campus. There's a nice horseshoe-shaped counter where you can sit. (That's where I sit, naturally, so I can ask the staff questions when they're not busy.) Open kitchen so you can watch them making the beautifully pungent pies. I always get 2 starter plates while I wait for the pizza: the Cantabrian anchovies and the chorizo. Nice wine list.

PIZZERIA VETRI
1939 Callowhill St, Philadelphia, 215-600-2629
www.pizzeriavetri.com
CUISINE: Pizza
DRINKS: Beer & Wine Only
SERVING: Lunch, Dinner
PRICE RANGE: $$
NEIGHBORHOOD: Fairmount
Dedicated solely to the art of making authentic Italian pizza, this place offers an impressive menu where almost everything is made from scratch. The menu includes a variety of seasonal pizza pies, thin curst and a thicker, rectangle-sized slice of the "pizza of the day." Also on the menu are roasted salads, calzones and the Rotolo, a crispy pinwheel of pizza filled with ricotta and mortadella topped with pistachio pesto. The bar serves a variety of wines and beers on tap.

RISTORANTE PANORAMA

Penn's View Inn Hotel, 14 N. Front St., 215-922-7800

www.pennsviewhotel.com/panorama

CUISINE: Italian

DRINKS: Full bar

SERVING: Mon – Fri lunch and dinner, Sat – Sun dinner only

PRICE RANGE: $$$

Authentic trattoria-style dining in the heart of Old City. The flavors of the Northern region influence this restaurant, with homemade pastas, authentic veal dishes, and fresh seafood specialties. A distinctive feature of Ristorante Panorama is their unique wine bar, **Il Bar**, with its custom-built, 120-bottle wine dispensing unit, the current Guinness Book of World Records holder. The restaurant's décor brings to mind the kind of place that should have been in the "Sopranos," with all the lavish Tuscan-inspired murals, stained glass windows, and over-the-top décor. In Il Bar, there's a reproduced mural of Titian's "Feast of Bacchus" and a dramatic wall of wine "on tap" behind the black granite bar. All you're waiting for is a couple of guys to come in with machines guns and kill everybody. Before they do, however, chow down on the Pappardelle al Sugo d'Anitra, homemade wide noodles in a slow-cooked ragout of duck; Scaloppine alla Zingara, thin veal medallions sautéed with house roasted red peppers and olives; and a variety of other pastas, antipasti selections and more.

ROUGE

205 S 18th St, Philadelphia, 215-732-6622

https://www.rouge98.com/
CUISINE: American (Traditional)
DRINKS: Full Bar
SERVING: Lunch & Dinner
PRICE RANGE: $$$
NEIGHBORHOOD: Rittenhouse
Popular sidewalk café known for American fare like classic burgers. Inside, at night it's got dim lighting that gives it a romantic feeling, much more so than at lunch. The big circular bar attracts a lot of people (that's where I sit). Menu picks: Baked Oysters (bacon, Calabrian chili butter, Pecorino crumbs) make for a very good starter—delicious; Crispy Chicken sandwich; Half chicken and Tuna Tartare.

SERPICO
604 South St, Philadelphia, 215-925-3001
www.serpicoonsouth.com
CUISINE: American; Pan-Asian

DRINKS: Full Bar
SERVING: Dinner
PRICE RANGE: $$$$
NEIGHBORHOOD: South Street District, Society Hill
This dark restaurant is headed by Chef Peter Serpico and Philly restaurateur Stephen Starr. Menu favorites include: Hand-torn pasta with snail sausage and Burnt onion mustard on Sliced Pig head. Great tasting menu.

SOUTHWARK
701 S 4th St, Philadelphia, 267-930-8538
www.southwarkrestaurant.com
CUISINE: American (New)
DRINKS: Full bar
SERVING: Dinner; closed Tues
PRICE RANGE: $$$
NEIGHBORHOOD: Queen Village
Handsome tavern setting with a menu of modern farm-to-table dishes. Modern farm-to-table dishes served alongside classic cocktails. Picks: Roasted Eggplant, smoked mackerel paté, menu changes often. Special late-night menu.

STEAP AND GRIND
1619 Frankford, Philadelphia, 267-858-4427
www.steapandgrind.com
CUISINE: Coffee, Tea
DRINKS: No Booze
SERVING: Sandwiches
PRICE RANGE: $
NEIGHBORHOOD: Fishtown

This is primarily a Coffee and Tea spot with a limited menu of sandwiches and snacks. Tea lovers take note—this place serves over 20 different varieties including caffeinated and herbal.

STEVE'S PRINCE OF STEAKS
7200 Bustleton Ave, 215-338-0985
www.stevesprinceofsteaks.com
CUISINE: Sandwiches/Cheesesteaks
DRINKS: No Booze
SERVING: Breakfast, Lunch, & Dinner
PRICE RANGE: $
NEIGHBORHOOD: Northeast
A meat eaters' paradise. Great steaks and sandwiches. Known for their cheesesteaks (could this be the famous Philly Cheesesteak?). What makes their cheesesteak so excellent is the high quality of the beef they use.

STOGIE JOE'S TAVERN
1801 E Passyunk Ave, Philadelphia, 215-463-3030
www.stogiejoestavern.net
CUISINE: Pub
DRINKS: Full Bar
SERVING: Lunch, & Dinner
PRICE RANGE: $$
NEIGHBOROOD: East Passyunk Crossing
Local tavern (sit outside when the weather's good) serving typical pub grub menu of pizza and sandwiches. Great Rigatoni Bolognese and cocktails. Check schedule for events like karaoke and live music. Cash only.

SURAYA

1528 Frankford Ave, Philadelphia, 215-302-1900
https://surayaphilly.com/
CUISINE: Lebanese
DRINKS: Full Bar
SERVING: Breakfast, Lunch & Dinner
PRICE RANGE: $$$
NEIGHBORHOOD: Fishtown

Chic café and market serving Lebanese cuisine in what used to be the gritty Fishtown area.. Colorful tile floors with a motif picked up and used in tiles behind the bar. Open kitchen behind bar lets you see what they're up to back there. The small "market" part of the place (offering handmade products and food items) is as busy as the restaurant part, with people bustling in and out, always a nice indication of popularity and quality. There's an enclosed outdoor patio / garden that's very pretty at night, with lights playing on the trees planted there. Menu picks: Beef kebab and Caledonia prawns. There's a wide variety of Lebanese specialties, but if you're not familiar with this cuisine, order the prix fixe meal—you get Hummous, Baba Ganoush, Muhammara, Labneh & Taboulé for the table to share; a choice of Mezza; Mashawi (choice of Kafta Kebab, Halabi Kebab Kawarma, Abu Sayf Baladi, Grilled Eggplant); and a choice of Dessert (Kanafeh, Coffee & Chocolate Verrine Tehina & Carob Mousse Glacèe Apples & Ashta). Very good vegetarian options. Great spot. You'll love it.

Jason Varney

TALULA'S GARDEN
210 W Washington Square, Philadelphia, 215-592-7787
www.talulasgarden.com
CUISINE: American
DRINKS: Full Bar
SERVING: Dinner; Sunday brunch from 10.
PRICE RANGE: $$$

NEIGHBORHOOD: Washington Square West
This unique restaurant offers an impressive menu of healthy American fare. Don't run away. It also TASTES good. There's a mural—really an inscription—on a portion of the wall above the seating area with a quote from legendary Chef Alice Waters: "A garden brings life and beauty to the table." You couldn't have a more spectacular temple to Alice's philosophy. The floor-to-ceiling windows in the bar allow lots of light in in the daytime, and the flashing headlights at night give the place a concentrated buzz. The outdoor areas are brimming with plants and excitement. My menu favorites include: torchon of foie gras and trout; crostini of chicken liver mousse, smoked sweet grapes, marinated mushrooms, crispy shallots, and watercress; rabbit sausage mixed in with pappardelle, fava beans, black olives, grana padano and rosemary; the succulent chicken under a brick, served with crispy Yukon gold potatoes and Castelvetrano olive, rustic bagnet vert herb-bread-caper sauce. Outdoor seating available in season and a nice bar area in back.

TINTO
114 S 20th St, Philadelphia, 215-665-9150
www.tintorestaurant.com
CUISINE: Tapas Bars
DRINKS: Full Bar
SERVING: Dinner
PRICE RANGE: $$$
NEIGHBORHOOD: Rittenhouse Square, Penn Center

Jose Garces is doing great things here at Tinto—try the tapas dish with sea bass and octopus with its nice citrus bite.

UPSTAIRS BAR AT THE FRANKLIN
112 S 18th St, 267-467-3277
www.thefranklinbar.com
NEIGHBORHOOD: Penn Center, Rittenhouse Square
Look for the unmarked entrance that leads to this popular subterranean cocktail bar. Upstairs, where it's more casual, the delightfully decorated Tiki bar serves classic Tiki cocktails. Décor is purposefully kitsch—cocktail umbrellas in the drinks, leis, string lighting, but this place (or rather these *two* places) are very professional. Custom cocktails made by pros.

Ashley Catharine Smith

VEDGE
1221 Locust St, Philadelphia, 215-320-7500
www.vedgerestaurant.com

CUISINE: Vegan, Vegetarian
DRINKS: Full Bar
SERVING: Dinner
PRICE RANGE: $$$
NEIGHBORHOOD: Washington Square West
Aptly named, this is a restaurant (opened in 2011) that celebrates vegetables. Husband & wife Chefs Richard Landau & Kate Jacoby offer a globally inspired menu featuring locally sourced ingredients in an elegant atmosphere. You'd never know it, but the truth is that no animal products are used in this kitchen. The dishes, however, are so flavorful, that you'd never be aware you were in a vegan restaurant if you weren't told. The craft cocktails that come from the bar are similarly creative, a rarity in most vegetarian/vegan eateries. Menu favorites include: Korean Seitan Taco; Cauliflower Soup; Braciole (smoked & roasted eggplant with Italian salsa verde; Grilled baby bok choy.

VERNICK FOOD & DRINK
2031 Walnut St, Philadelphia, 267-639-6644
www.vernickphilly.com
CUISINE: American
DRINKS: Full Bar
SERVING: Dinner
PRICE RANGE: $$$
NEIGHBORHOOD: Rittenhouse Square, Penn Center
Creative American fare with Asian touches served as small and large plates meant for sharing.

VETRI
1312 Spruce St, Philadelphia, 215-732-3478

www.vetricucina.com
CUISINE: Italian
DRINKS: Full Bar
SERVING: Dinner
PRICE RANGE: $$$$
NEIGHBORHOOD: Washington Square West,
Avenue of the Arts, South
Marc Vetric is widely admired (even by a lot of other
chefs) for his excellent pasta dishes.

VILLA DI ROMA
936 S 9th St, Philadelphia, 215-592-1295
www.villadiroma.com
CUISINE: Italian
DRINKS: Full Bar
SERVING: Dinner
PRICE RANGE: $$
NEIGHBORHOOD: Italian Market, Bella Vista
A no-frills, down-home place. I could live on the
linguine with clams (white sauce, of course), and the
eggplant parmesan is almost as good as my mother's.

VOLVÉR

Kimmel Center for the Performing Arts
300 S Broad St, Philadelphia, 215-670-2302
www.volverrestaurant.com
CUISINE: Tapas/Small Plates
DRINKS: Full Bar
SERVING: Dinner; closed Mon & Tues
PRICE RANGE: $$$$
NEIGHBOROOD: Rittenhouse Square
Chef Jose Garces offers tasting menus (8 courses or 12) of some of his favorite dishes that have been re-imagined for this eatery. Inspired by international flavors, Chef Garces creates regional specialties from locally sourced products. Nice wine selection.

WALNUT STREET CAFÉ

2929 Walnut St, 215-867-8067
www.walnutstreetcafe.com
CUISINE: American Traditional
DRINKS: Full Bar
SERVING: Breakfast, Lunch, & Dinner
PRICE RANGE: $$
NEIGHBORHOOD: University City
Popular café serving American fare with a pastry counter in a delightful setting with marble tables, pastel-colored dishes and flowers everwhere. Simple menu. Great choice for weekend brunch. Try the Salmon Eggs Benedict, Cherry and pistachio croissant. Cocktail bar.

WILL BYOB

1911 E Passyunk, Philadelphia, 215-271-7683
www.willbyob.com
CUISINE: American, French
DRINKS: No Booze, but BYOB is OK
SERVING: Dinner Wednesday-Sunday; closed
Monday & Tuesday
PRICE RANGE: $$$
NEIGHBORHOOD: South Philadelphia
This French inspired restaurant operating in a tiny
(and somewhat noisy) space offers a nice menu of
classic dishes. Menu favorites include: English pea
gazpacho; Burgundy-style snails, with new potatoes,
chicken liver and curds & whey; Hudson Valley foie
gras & rabbit terrine; Whole Roasted Hen; Duck
Breast with lavender spices. They offer a Sunday pix
fixe and Tuesday tasting menu. As the name suggest,
you have to bring your own wine.

WM. MULHERIN'S SONS

1355 N Front St, 215-291-1355

www.wmmulherinssons.com
CUISINE: Italian
DRINKS: Full Bar
SERVING: Dinner, Lunch on Sat & Sun
PRICE RANGE: $$$
NEIGHBORHOOD: Fishtown

Popular Italian eatery featuring dark woods, brick walls, a cozy atmosphere, very clubby, reclaimed timber ceilings, all created in a building that used to house a whiskey blending and bottling plant. In cold weather, try to get a couple of chairs by the fireside—they'll serve you food right there on the low tables. Creative menu. Try the blistered Speck pizza with an egg on top or the Hanger Steak. Nice selection of pastas (like tortellini with rabbit, mortadella and pistachios). Great brunch spot. Reservations recommended. By the way, there's a hotel upstairs with 4 very nicely restored rooms, so this makes a great place to stay while you visit.

ZAHAV

237 St James Pl, Philadelphia, 215-625-8800
www.zahavrestaurant.com
CUISINE: Middle Eastern
DRINKS: Full Bar
SERVING: Dinner
PRICE RANGE: $$
NEIGHBORHOOD: Society Hill

Chef Michael Solomonov offers a menu featuring Israeli-Mediterranean cuisine. ZAHAV means "gold" in Hebrew. With the décor here, they tried to emulate the hidden courtyards of Jerusalem, with golden limestone floors and walls, hard-carved tables and soaring ceilings. You'll start out with the "laffa" bread (a kind of flatbread), baked to order in their wood-burning "Taboon oven." The restaurant offers a casual dining experience but a memorable one. Menu favorites include: Chicken Shishlik; sizzling skewers of meat grilled over hardwood charcoal; Spiced Eggplant. There's quite a variety of different cuisines represented, from Israel to Eastern Europe to North Africa and Persia. Altogether one of the more interesting places in Philadelphia.

Chapter 5
WHAT TO SEE & DO

9TH STREET ITALIAN MARKET VISITOR CENTER
919 S 9th St, Philadelphia, 215-278-2903
www.italianmarketphilly.org
NEIGHBORHOOD: Italian Market, Bella Vista
This open-air market has been in Philadelphia
forever. It is still strongly ethnic, not just Italian.
There are Koreans, Indians and Pakistanis.

BARNES FOUNDATION MUSEUM

2025 Benjamin Franklin Pkwy, Philadelphia: 215-278-7000

www.barnesfoundation.org

ADMISSION: Admission is expensive, over $40.

For most of its 90-year history, the Barnes Foundation Museum was seven miles away in suburban Merion. But after years of controversy and construction, it relocated, bringing one of the world's great collections of works by Picasso, Matisse and Modigliani (and many others) to Museum Row. On Friday nights, the otherwise somber space hosts concerts and pours wine until 10 p.m.

BENJAMIN FRANKLIN MUSEUM

317 Chestnut St, Philadelphia, 267-514-1522

www.nps.gov/inde/planyourvisit/benjaminfranklinmuseum.htm

HOURS: Open daily except for major holidays.

ADMISSION: Nominal fee

This unique museum is dedicated to Philadelphia's founding father, and in my opinion, the most interesting of all the American founders. Museum is stuffed with artifacts and exhibits, computer animations and interactive displays, all celebrating Franklin's fascinatingly rich life and wide ranging achievements. Individual exhibits show the different aspects of Franklin's life.

BRANDYWINE RIVER MUSEUM
1 Hoffman's Mill Rd, Chadds Ford, 610-388-2700
www.brandywinemuseum.org
Right outside the city, this museum is their temple to the Wyeth family. You see the work in the settings where they were painted. Bring lunch and eat it by the Brandywine River.

CARPENTERS' HALL
320 Chestnut St, Philadelphia, 215-925-0167
www.carpentershall.org
NEIGHBORHOOD: Old City
ADMISSION: Free; closed Mondays
This two-story brick building is noted as a key meeting place in history acting as the oldest trade guild in America, since 1770. This hall hosted the First Continental Congress in 1774 and was home to Franklin's Library Company, The American Philosophical Society, and the First and Second Banks of the United States. The Hall welcomes over 150,000 world-wide visitors annually.

CITIZENS BANK PARK
1 Citizens Bank Way, Philadelphia, 215-463-1000
http://philadelphia.phillies.mlb.com/phi/ballpark/infor
mation/index.jsp
Philly is one of the great sports towns of America.
My movie partner Beau Rogers lives there on the
Main Line and when I go north from Miami, he
always takes me to the Phillies, Eagles, 76ers, etc. I
used to play baseball, so I simply love watching
baseball games. This park offers something else
besides the game, though—spectacular views toward
the city.

EASTERN STATE PENITENTIARY HISTORIC SITE
2027 Fairmount Ave, Philadelphia, 215-236-3300
NEIGHBORHOOD: Fairmount, Art Museum District
www.EasternState.org

A jail that's been turned into a museum. This isn't just any old jail that's fallen on hard times. It has Gothic towers, turrets and Al Capone's (by standards at the time) luxurious cell. A very interesting way to spend the afternoon. A very interesting way to spend the afternoon, especially when it's raining outside and you can't enjoy the city the way it was meant to be enjoyed and best absorbed—by walking.

FAIRMOUNT PARK
1 Boathouse Row, Philadelphia, 215-988-9334
www.visitphilly.com/outdoor-
activities/philadelphia/fairmount-park/
A splendid, 9,200-acre park with broad-stroked English-style landscapes. When you drive along the river, you'll see jaw-dropping views.

INDEPENDENCE NATIONAL HISTORICAL PARK
143 S 3rd St, Philadelphia, 215-965-2305

NEIGHBORHOOD: Old City
www.nps.gov/inde/
One of Philadelphia's main attractions. Its 18th Century Garden is about midway between the Fifth Street and Second Street subway stations. The National Park Service now operates a portrait gallery in the Greek Revival-style Second Bank of the United States, located in Independence National Historical Park.

INDEPENDENCE SEAPORT MUSEUM
211 South Christopher Columbus Boulevard, Philadelphia, 215-413-8655
www.phillyseaport.org
HOURS: Open daily
ADMISSION: Moderate fee
Museum mainly dedicated to the maritime history of Philadelphia and surrounding ports along the Delaware River. Filled with art, artifacts, historical ships, and archival materials celebrating the maritime history of the Greater Delaware Valley and other major regional ports.

INSTITUTE OF CONTEMPORARY ART
118 S 36th St, Philadelphia, 215-898-7108
www.icaphila.org
NEIGHBORHOOD: Universal City
ADMISSION: Free; closed Monday & Tuesday
Located on the campus of the University of Pennsylvania, this museum focuses on contemporary art created by living artists. The museum hosts performances, lectures, and readings.

MANAYUNK
www.manayunk.com
This area is like a small town within the city. Walk the towpath along the canal, where Philadelphia's industry started, to see romantic ruins and chic renovations of mill buildings. Sample Main Street's many stores and restaurants. There's no mall here—just a big open sky.

MARIO LANZA INSTITUTE AND MUSEUM
712 Montrose St, Philadelphia, 215-238-9691
www.mariolanzainstitute.org
HOURS: Open Mon, Tues, Fri & Sat
ADMISSION: Nominal fee
Institute and museum honors the memory of the great singer Mario Lanza. My mother played Lanza's records constantly, so I grew up listing to his renditions from "The Student Prince" and the other operettas he starred in. Museum features photos and

artifacts including clothing worn by Lanza, original movie posters, and some of his gold records.

THE MUSEUM OF THE AMERICAN REVOLUTION
101 South Third St, Philadelphia, 215-253-6731
www.amrevmuseum.org
NEIGHBORHOOD: Old City
ADMISSION: Nominal Fee; open every day
A mecca for scholars and aficionados of the American Revolution, this museum boasts a distinguished collection of artwork, sculpture, textiles, weapons, manuscripts and rare books. The American Revolution is brought to life in the many exhibition galleries, theaters and large-scale tableaux. This museum is also a portal to other Revolutionary landmarks. You can see General Washington's field tent where he lived and worked from 1778-1783. It's a linen tent that runs 23 feet long by 14 feet wide. (It was held previously by the Valley Forge Historical Society.) You can also see evidence of slavery, with a pair of shackles small enough to restrain a child. Also, Washington's silver cups he took when in the field.

NATIONAL CONSTITUTION CENTER
Independence Mall, 525 Arch St., Philadelphia: 215-409-6600
www.constitutioncenter.org
Admission fee.
The National Constitution Center is the first and only nonprofit, nonpartisan museum devoted to the Constitution and its legacy of freedom. Curated by

Daniel Okrent, author of a best-selling book on the Prohibition era, the exhibition here has flapper dresses, temperance propaganda, a 1929 Buick Marquette and original copies of the 18th and 21st Amendments.

PENNSYLVANIA ACADEMY OF FINE ARTS
118-128 N Broad St, Philadelphia, 215-972-7600
www.pafa.org
NEIGHBORHOOD: Penn Center, Logan Square, Avenue of the Arts North
www.pafa.org
This is a beautiful example of 19th-century architect Frank Furness's work. His buildings are among my favorites. They fit together with the same articulation as machines

PENNSYLVANIA HOSPITAL
800 Spruce Street Philadelphia, 215-829-3000
www.pennmedicine.org/for-patients-and-visitors/penn-medicine-locations/pennsylvania-hospital
NEIGHBORHOOD: Washington Square West
SELF-GUIDED TOURS: Small Fee
This private, non-profit 534-bed teaching hospital is the oldest hospital in America. Founded in 1751 by Benjamin Franklin and Dr. Thomas Bond, this building is steeped in history and unlike many working hospitals offers tours. Highlights for the tour include the historical library and the lecture amphitheater on the third floor. Self-guided tour (inquire at the Welcome Desk, located first floor, Preston Building, at 8th and Spruce). Guided tours are also available Mon-Fri 9 am-4:30 pm. Contact at least

48 hours in advance for a guided tour. Guided tours are subject to the availability of tour guides. 215-829-8796

PHILADELPHIA MURAL ARTS PROGRAM
1729 Mt Vernon St, Philadelphia, 215-685-0750
www.muralarts.org
You can tour "The World's Largest Outdoor Art Gallery" by foot or by trolley, but it's really something you ought to do on your first trip to Philadelphia. It's all part of the city's Mural Arts Program that includes more than 600 murals.

PHILADELPHIA MUSEUM OF ART
2600 Benjamin Franklin Pkwy, Philadelphia: 215-763-8100
www.philamuseum.org
Admission fee.
One of the largest art museums in the U.S. with collections of more than 227,000 objects including

world-class holdings of European and American paintings, prints, drawings and decorative arts. Don't miss "The Life Line" by Winslow Homer.

PHILADELPHIA NAVY YARD
4747 S Broad St, Philadelphia, 215-THE-YARD
www.navyyard.org
Offers a different waterfront view and can be reached by taking the Broad Street subway line and then the 71 bus.

PLEASE TOUCH MUSEUM
4231 Ave of the Republic, Philadelphia, 215-581-3181
www.pleasetouchmuseum.org
A beautiful, state-of-the-art museum for children, located in historic Memorial Hall.

RITTENHOUSE SQUARE
18th and Walnut Streets Philadelphia, 215-636-1666
www.visitphilly.com/museums-attractions/philadelphia/rittenhouse-square-park

Built during the booming 1850s, the Rittenhouse Square neighborhood was home to the city's Victorian aristocracy. The park has a reflecting pool, diagonal walkways crisscrossing beneath oak, maple and locust trees, and bronze sculptures, like the 1832 allegory of the French Revolution, "Lion Crushing a Serpent," by Antoine-Louis Barye.

SCHUYLKILL BANKS
2401 Walnut St, Philadelphia: 215-309-5523
www.schuylkillbanks.org
Schuylkill Banks, the city's 1.2-mile-long waterfront trail, is Philadelphia's most recent riverfront destination with greenways, parks, docks, the nation's leading educational institutions, award-winning residential developments and active industrial sites that are making way for livable spaces.

SCHUYLKILL RIVER TRAIL
Philadelphia Section, Philadelphia, 215-683-0200
NEIGHBORHOOD: Manayunk, Roxborough
www.schuylkillrivertrail.com/index.php
This is the Best Bike Path in town that runs along the river that leads out to Kelly Drive. When you ride here, you'll see runners, pedestrians and the city skyline.

VALLEY FORGE NATIONAL HISTORICAL PARK

1400 N Outer Line Drive, King of Prussia, 610-783-1000

www.nps.gov/vafo

Go in winter so you can see where Washington suffered along with his troops. From downtown Philadelphia, take the 125 bus. Be warned if you arrive sans car: the shuttle that takes you around the park operates on a seasonal basis.

WALKING TOUR

ushistory.org/more/mauger

215-627-8680

Ed Mauger (who wrote the book "Philadelphia Then & Now") offers custom history and architecture walking tours. He's a lot of fun and full of so much interesting historical facts. Well worth your time.

WANAMAKER EAGLE STATUE
1300 Market St, Philadelphia, No Phone
www.associationforpublicart.org/artwork/eagle/
You'll want to visit the Great Court at the center of
the old Wanamaker's department store (it's now a
Macy's). This is the store that typified Philadelphia
the way Marshall Field's meant Chicago. The whole
city shopped here. (Well, if you had any money.) The
famous organ is still there in all its glory. People still
drift in at Christmas to hear the music.

Chapter 6
SHOPPING & SERVICES

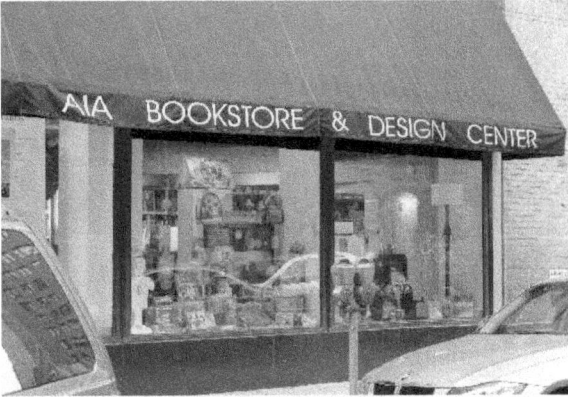

AIA BOOKSTORE & DESIGN CENTER
1218 Arch St, Philadelphia, 215-569-3188
NEIGHBORHOOD: Market East
www.aiabookstore.com
They have not only books, but interesting things that can be good souvenirs. Last time I was there, I found cute, colorful kitchen tools.

CAPOGIRO GELATO ARTISANS
119 South 13th St., Philadelphia: 215-351-0900
www.capogirogelato.com
They make 27 flavors fresh each morning. Try the lime cilantro or the cranberry apple.

CENTER FOR ART IN WOOD
141 North Third St., Philadelphia: 215-923-8000
www.centerforartinwood.org
Afterward, window-shop along Third Street, where vintage boutiques vie for your attention. Don't miss the Center for Art in Wood, a gallery and store devoted to wood-centric creativity.

DI BRUNO BROS
1730 Chestnut St, Philadelphia, 215-665-9220
www.dibruno.com
NEIGHBORHOOD: Rittenhouse Square/Penn Center
Known as "The House of Cheese," this shop offers
over 300 types of cheeses year round. The gourmet
food store offers a wide variety of specialty foods,
seafood, kosher meats, and a charcuterie counter. The
coffee bar serves La Colombe coffees beginning at 7
a.m. with freshly made bagels and baked goods. If
you're hungry, visit the Upstairs @ Di Bruno – open
for lunch and weekend brunch.

ISGRO PASTRIES
1009 Christian St, Philadelphia, 215-923-3092
www.bestcannoli.com
Delicious sfogliatella (if you don't know what that is,
you need to go and find out).

JOAN SHEPP BOUTIQUE
1811 Chestnut, Philadelphia, 215-735-2666
www.joanshepp.com
Collections of designer clothing.

JOSEPH FOX BOOKSHOP
1724 Sansom St., Philadelphia: 215-563-4184
https://www.foxbookshop.com/
This bookstore has been a part of Philadelphia since
1951. It's a joy to browse among the bookshelves
packed with every imaginable type of book. Attracts
many authors when they tour.

THE PARLOUR
1339 Frankford, Philadelphia, 215-278-7613

www.theparlourfishtown.com
NEIGHBORHOOD: Fishtown
This industrial-chic hair and skin salon pampers you
like no other salon. You're offered a cocktail when
you enter and treated like a VIP during the entire
experience. If you're there for a cut or a styling, the
shampoo girl also massages your head and neck
during the shampoo. Services include: Ayurvedic
organic facials, custom razor cuts, and massages.

POLLYODD
1908 E Passyunk Ave, Philadelphia, 215-271-1161
www.pollyodd.com
Philadelphia-based distillery Naoj & Mot, Inc offers a
variety of Italian-American liqueurs. Known for their
popular Pollyodd Lemoncello and Pollyodd
Chocolatecello flavors. This is the first female owned
Distillery in the country.

READING TERMINAL MARKET
51 N 12th St, Philadelphia, 215-922-2317
NEIGHBORHOOD: Market East
www.readingterminalmarket.org

Hop on the Market-Frankford subway line that stops at the nearby 11th Street and 13th Street stations. You can find various types of cheeses and interesting olive oils at Salumeria and Downtown Cheese. You should also try Pennsylvania Dutch-influenced food, such as German meats at Smucker's Quality Meats.

TERMINI BROS BAKERY
1523 S 8th St, Philadelphia, 215-334-1816
www.termini.com
Their flagship store. Chocolate-chip cannoli and pignoli-nut cookies.

VERDE
108 South 13th St., Philadelphia: 215-546-8700
www.verdephiladelphia.com
Look out for charm bracelets, other jewelry,
accessories and gift, women's clothing by
international designers, patent leather bags and
artisanal Marcie Blaine chocolates which are worth
the trip alone.

INDEX

90

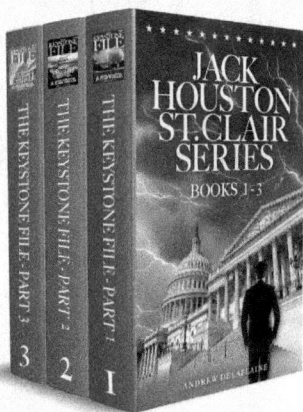

WANT 3 **FREE** THRILLERS?

Why, of course you do!

If you like these writers--
Vince Flynn, Brad Thor, Tom Clancy, James
Patterson, David Baldacci, John Grisham,
Brad Meltzer, Daniel Silva, Don DeLillo

If you like these TV series –
House of Cards, Scandal, West Wing, The
Good Wife, Madam Secretary, Designated
Survivor

You'll love the **unputdownable** series about
Jack Houston St. Clair, with political intrigue, romance,
and loads of action and suspense.

Besides writing travel books, I've written political thrillers for many years that have delighted hundreds of thousands of readers. I want to introduce you to my work!
Send me an email and I'll send you a link where you can download the first 3 books in my bestselling series, absolutely FREE.

Mention **this book** when you email me.

andrewdelaplaine@mac.com

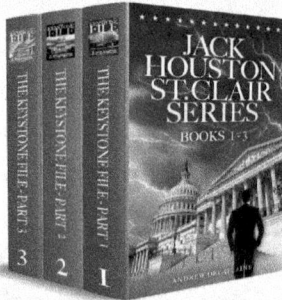